How to Draw
Awesome
Vehicles
and Amazing Trucks

Green Android

Created and produced by Green Android Ltd

Illustrated by Fiona Gowen

Green Android Ltd
49 Beaumont Court
Upper Clapton Road
London E5 8BG
United Kingdom
www.greenandroid.co.uk

ISBN 978-1-909244-26-9

Printed and bound in Dongguan, China, May 2014

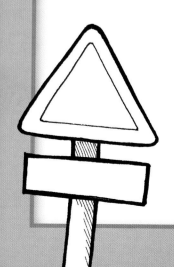

Contents

 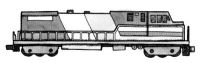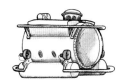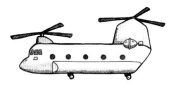
Page 32 has an index of everything to draw in this book.

How to Draw

Huge Haulers

Big rigs are used to haul heavy freight from one place to another. Some of these trucks are so powerful they can pull several trailers at once.

HEAVY LOAD

STOP

1 Start your picture by drawing the truck's three large wheels.

2 You can now draw the base and wheel arch of the truck. Add a rectangle for the fuel tank.

3 Now draw an outline for the cab and the exhaust pipe.

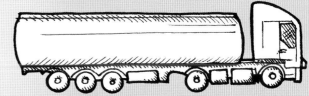

Add the driver's window to the cab and some windows to the above-cab sleeping compartment.

Add some detail to your drawing, such as air inlets on the bonnet and panels on the side of the cab.

Big rig

To finish your drawing, add some shading to the areas of the truck that are in shadow.

Fuel tanker

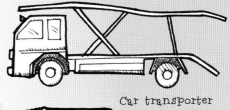

Car transporter

Concrete mixer

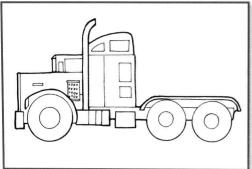

Low loader

Road train

Tipper truck

Delivery truck

Log transporter

WIDE VEHICLE

Rubbish truck

How to Draw

Super Racers

Nothing beats the noise and excitement of a race track. Formula One racing is a fast and dangerous motor sport, where drivers need nerves of steel!

1 Start your race car picture by drawing a pair of wheels.

2 Draw two parallel lines connecting the two wheels. This is the base of your car.

3 Now draw the outline of the race car between the two wheels.

More to Draw

Racing vehicles come in all shapes and sizes, from the smallest kart to enormous racing trucks.

Street racer

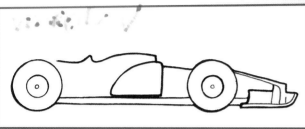

Dragster

4 Draw the long, thin bonnet of the race car onto the front of the right-hand wheel.

Stock car

Off-road racer

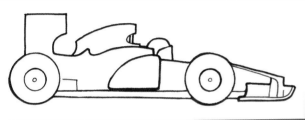

5 Now you can add the helmet of the driver, the engine intake behind the driver and the large rear wing.

Speedway racer

Rally car

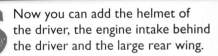

Formula One car

Truck racer

6 To finish the drawing, go over the lines and add some shading. This will help give it a realistic look.

Superkart

Endurance racer

Fantastic Builders

Construction sites are amazing places where machines haul, dig and lift materials. This roller is used to flatten the ground when making roads.

1 Draw a rear wheel with a rectangle through it and smaller back wheel.

2 You can now join the two wheels together by drawing the base of the cab.

3 Draw the cab onto the base. Add windows for the driver to see through.

4 Draw the engine cover and exhaust pipe onto the back of the roller.

Backhoe loader

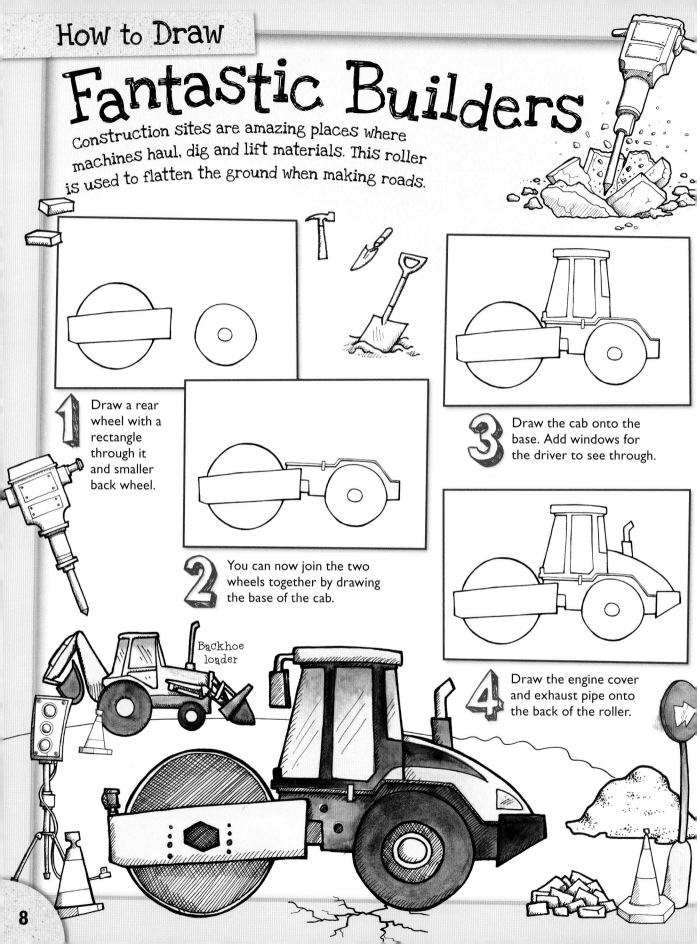

More to Draw

Here are some more working vehicles that you could add to drawings of construction sites.

Bulldozer

Tele-handler

5 Add the wing mirror and some lights. Add details to the roller's body such as rivets and panels.

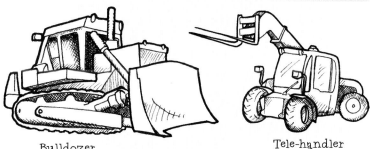

Grader

Forklift

Roller

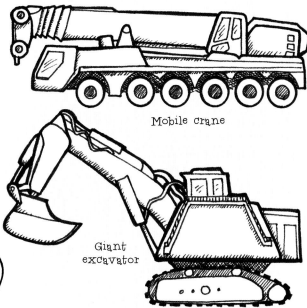

Mobile crane

Giant excavator

6 Finish your drawing of a roller by shading some areas and adding lnes for reflections onto the windows.

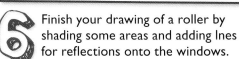

Mini excavator

Giant dump truck

9

How to Draw

Extreme Supercars

Supercars are some of the fastest and most stylish cars. These exotic cars offer incredible performance on the road or the race track.

START

1 Start your supercar drawing with two circles for the wheels.

2 Now you can draw the outline of the supercar around the two wheels.

3 Add the car's window, door and wheel arch to the drawing.

Gumpert Apollo

Koenigsegg Agera R

4 Add details for the lights, mirror, seat, door handle and air inlets on the side of the car.

Bugatti Veyron SS

5 Add a small circle at each wheel's centre and the spokes.

6 Finish your drawing by going over the main lines again and then adding some shading to the car.

Lamborghini Aventador LP700

McLaren F1

Saleen S7

To the Rescue

Rescue vehicles are amazing machines that help the rescue teams to perform their life-saving jobs as quickly and safely as possible.

1 Start your drawing with the outline of the ladder.

2 You can now add the outline of the fire engine underneath the ladder.

3 Draw shapes connecting the engine to the ladder, then add a bumper and wheels.

4 Draw the details for the ladder and then add the apparatus and dials onto the engine.

More to Draw

There are many different sorts of rescue vehicles.
They are designed to perform specific tasks.

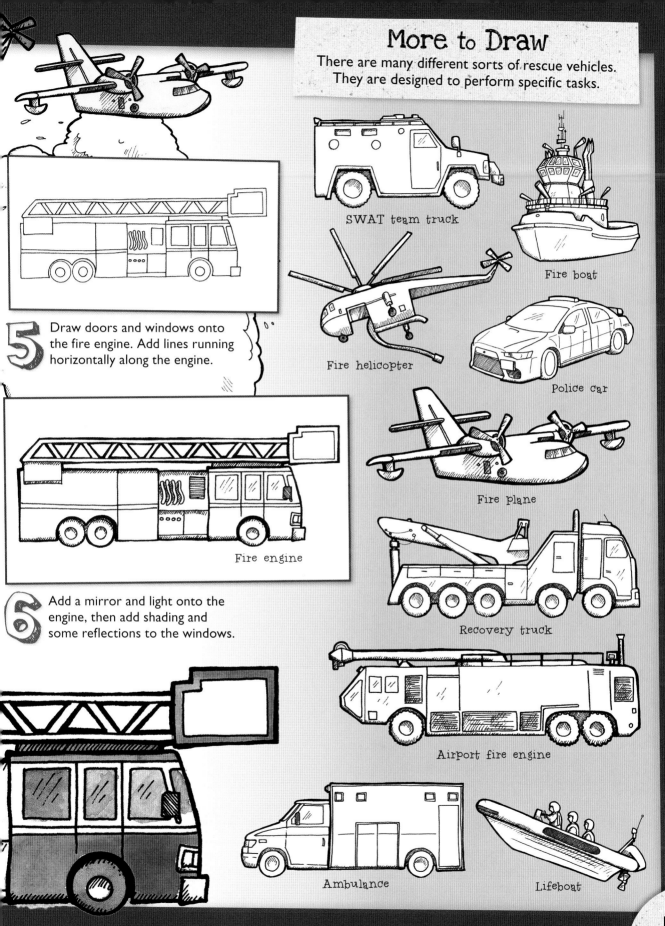

5 Draw doors and windows onto the fire engine. Add lines running horizontally along the engine.

Fire engine

6 Add a mirror and light onto the engine, then add shading and some reflections to the windows.

SWAT team truck

Fire boat

Fire helicopter

Police car

Fire plane

Recovery truck

Airport fire engine

Ambulance

Lifeboat

How to Draw
Mighty Trains

Railways were built all over the world to carry people and goods. Trains have evolved from early steam-powered engines to high-speed bullet trains.

Double decker train

1 Draw the thin base and the outline of the train engine.

2 You can now add two sets of wheels underneath the base of the train.

3 Draw lines inside the train to separate out the different sections of the train.

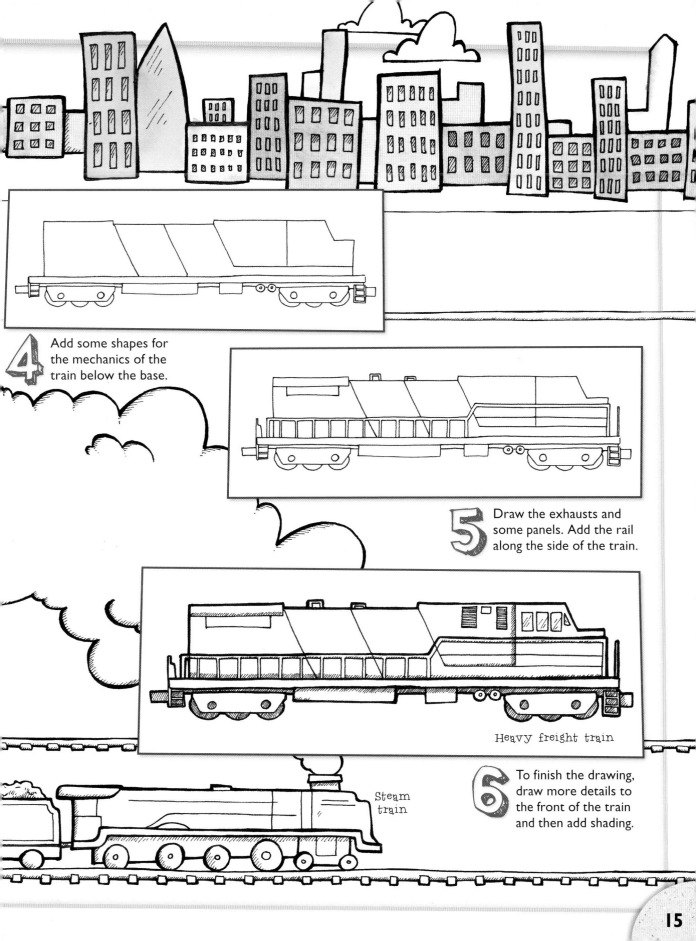

4 Add some shapes for the mechanics of the train below the base.

5 Draw the exhausts and some panels. Add the rail along the side of the train.

Heavy freight train

Steam train

6 To finish the drawing, draw more details to the front of the train and then add shading.

Groovy Bikes

Riding bikes can be a fast way to travel around. From pedal power to high-speed motorbikes, travelling on two wheels is always a lot of fun.

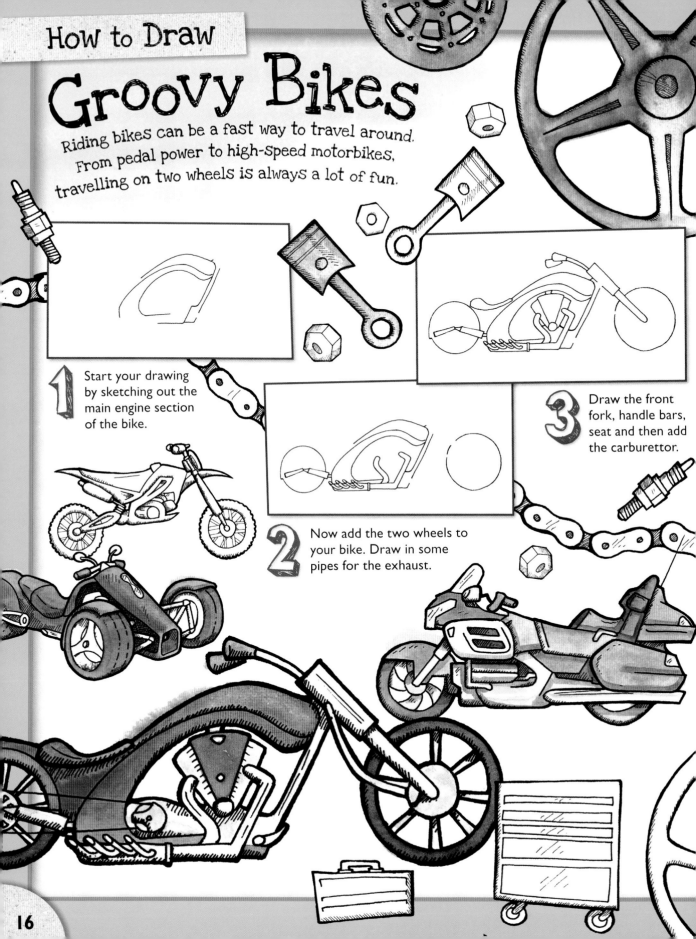

1 Start your drawing by sketching out the main engine section of the bike.

2 Now add the two wheels to your bike. Draw in some pipes for the exhaust.

3 Draw the front fork, handle bars, seat and then add the carburettor.

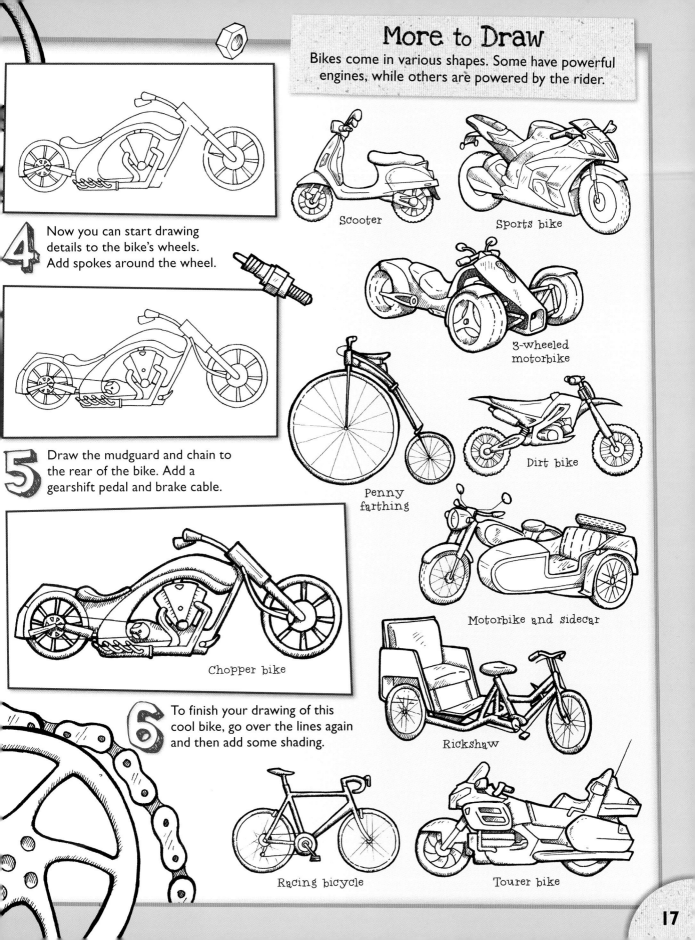

Bikes come in various shapes. Some have powerful engines, while others are powered by the rider.

4 Now you can start drawing details to the bike's wheels. Add spokes around the wheel.

5 Draw the mudguard and chain to the rear of the bike. Add a gearshift pedal and brake cable.

6 To finish your drawing of this cool bike, go over the lines again and then add some shading.

Scooter

Sports bike

3-wheeled motorbike

Penny farthing

Dirt bike

Motorbike and sidecar

Chopper bike

Rickshaw

Racing bicycle

Tourer bike

17

Rugged Racers

Monster trucks are customised pick-up trucks with huge wheels. They are used for racing, jumping and doing cool tricks at truck shows.

1 Draw two large wheels. Add two circles in each wheel.

2 Join the wheels together with some lines. This will become the suspension.

3 Now you can add an outline for the truck's cab and bed.

4 Now add different support bars and struts to make this truck very strong and safe.

Monster truck

6 Finish your drawing by going over the lines again and then adding some shading.

5 Add details to the cab such as a window, steering wheel and door. Decorate the tyres of the truck.

How to Draw

Off-roaders

Off-road vehicles are designed to travel over rough or unusual terrain. These exciting vehicles don't let anything get in their way!

1 Draw two large wheels. Now add two circles inside each wheel.

2 Now draw an outline for the off-roader. Draw a line for each wheel arch.

3 Draw the doors and then the windows. Also add a panel for the roof and lid of the boot.

4 Draw the bull bars at the front of the vehicle and the side step bars on the undercarriage.

More to Draw
All of these vehicles are designed to travel off road.
These can be added to drawings of rugged scenery.

Quad bike

Crawler tractor

Tractor

Dune buggy

5 Add details for all the panels,
hinges, air inlets and fuel cap.
Decorate the wheels and tyres.

Off-road Hummer

Off-road camper

6 Finish your drawing by going over
the lines once more and then
adding shading and reflections.

Amphibious car

Snow cat

Jeep

Pick-up truck

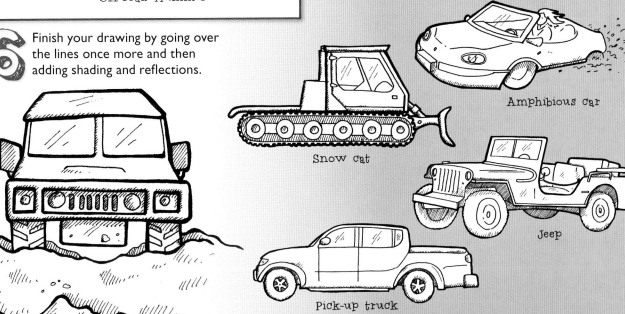

How to Draw
On the Water

People have used boats to travel on water for thousands of years. Some boats carry cargo, others are used for racing and some are sailed just for fun.

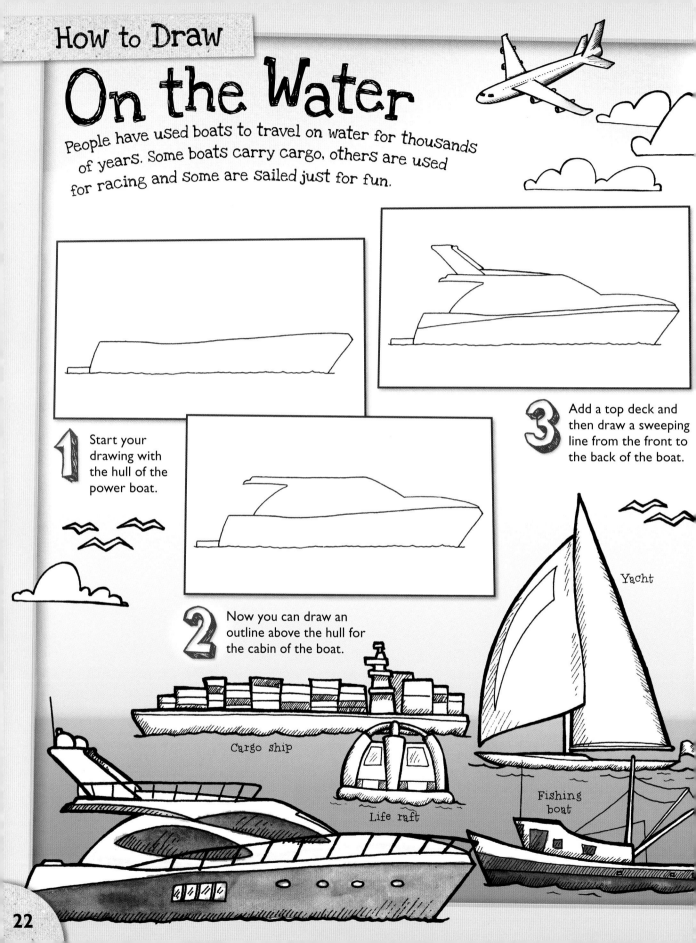

1 Start your drawing with the hull of the power boat.

2 Now you can draw an outline above the hull for the cabin of the boat.

3 Add a top deck and then draw a sweeping line from the front to the back of the boat.

Yacht

Cargo ship

Life raft

Fishing boat

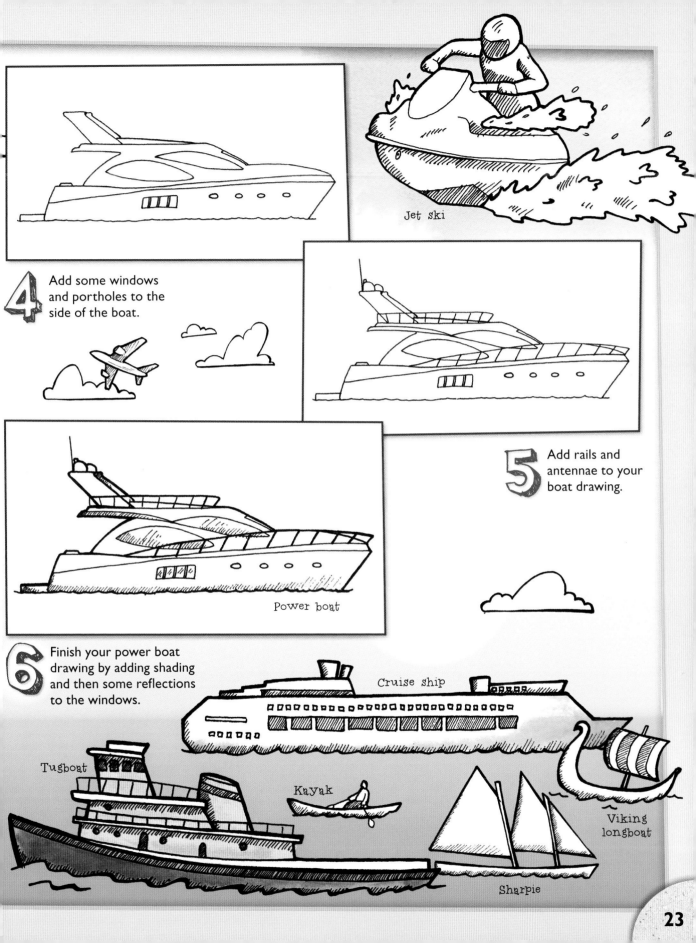

Jet ski

4 Add some windows and portholes to the side of the boat.

5 Add rails and antennae to your boat drawing.

Power boat

6 Finish your power boat drawing by adding shading and then some reflections to the windows.

Cruise ship

Tugboat

Kayak

Viking longboat

Sharpie

Underwater Explorers

Some vehicles are designed to travel under the water. These vehicles are used for research and for making repairs to underwater pipelines.

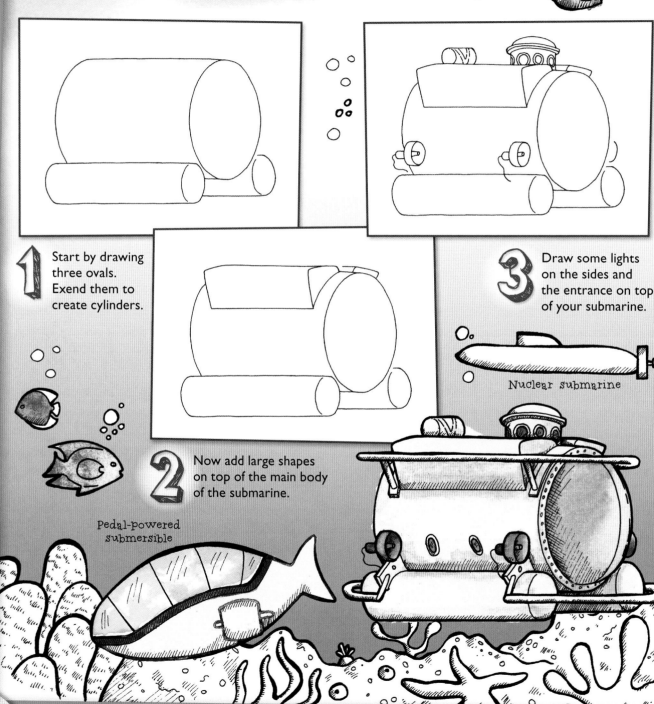

1 Start by drawing three ovals. Exend them to create cylinders.

2 Now add large shapes on top of the main body of the submarine.

3 Draw some lights on the sides and the entrance on top of your submarine.

Nuclear submarine

Pedal-powered submersible

Remote control
underwater camera

4 You can now add both of the safety rails to your submarine.

One-man mini submersible

5 Draw two portholes onto the side of the submarine.

Underwater car

Deep-sea submersible

6 Finish your drawing by shading in areas and adding rivets.

How to Draw

In the Sky

There are many ways that we can fly through the air, from simple hang gliders and hot-air balloons to super-fast jet-propelled planes and helicopters.

Hang glider

Spy plane

1 Start your drawing with the outline of a helicopter.

2 Now draw a shape for the side panel on the helicopter and the engine cover on the tail.

3 Add a shape on the front of the helicopter. This is where the rotor transmission is housed.

4 You can now add two sets of rotary blades onto each end of the helicopter body.

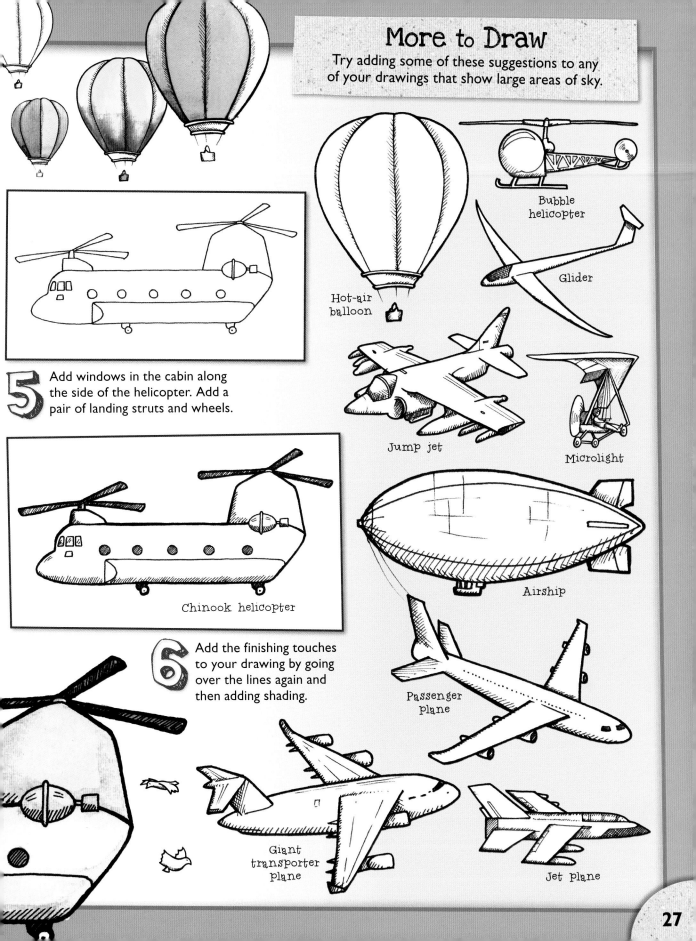

More to Draw
Try adding some of these suggestions to any
of your drawings that show large areas of sky.

5 Add windows in the cabin along the side of the helicopter. Add a pair of landing struts and wheels.

Chinook helicopter

6 Add the finishing touches to your drawing by going over the lines again and then adding shading.

Hot-air balloon

Bubble helicopter

Glider

Jump jet

Microlight

Airship

Passenger plane

Giant transporter plane

Jet plane

How to Draw
Aerobatic Fliers

Areobatic planes have been designed to show off the pilot's skills in flying. At some air shows, large groups of these planes will fly in perfect unison.

1 Start by drawing the nose. This is a cone inside a rectangle.

2 Now draw the outline of the plane. Leave gaps for the wing to be added.

3 Now you can draw the wings onto the side of the plane.

Triplane

Biplane

4 Now draw the cockpit, window and landing gear.

Stunt plane

5 Add some striped shapes down the length of the wings and along the side of the body of your plane.

6 To finish your drawing, go over the lines once again and then add some shading and reflections.

Jet trainer

Futuristic Travellers

Inventors are looking at new ways to improve our transport systems. We can only guess at how people may travel in the future.

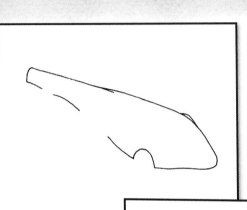

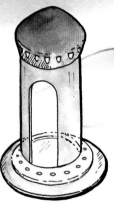

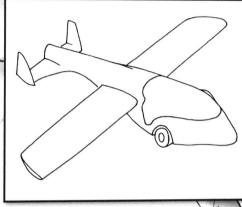

1 Start with the skycar's outline. Leave gaps for the wings.

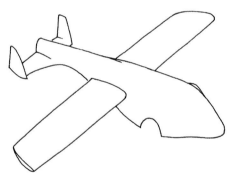

2 Add the wings at the side of the plane and the rudder and stabiliser at the back.

3 Draw a window around the cockpit and then add the wheel to your plane.

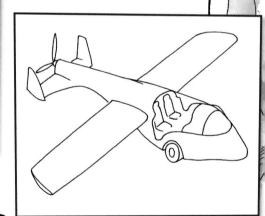

4 Now draw some details in the cockpit and add a propeller to the back of the plane's tail.

Here are some examples of future vehicles that engineers and designers are currently working on.

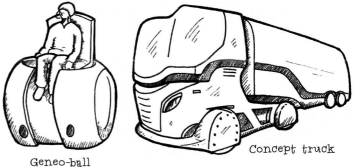

Geneo-ball

Concept truck

Solar yacht

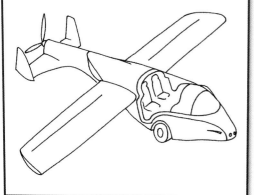

5 Add detail to the bodywork of the plane with lines around the cockpit, nose and along the wings.

Cosmic tractor

Teleportation device

Skycar

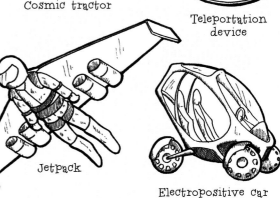

Jetpack

Electropositive car

6 Finish your drawing by shading some of the areas to give a realistic look to your plane.

Concept car

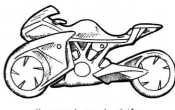

Concept motorbike

Vehicle Index

There are over one hundred different vehicles in this book. Practice your new-found drawing skills by adding some of them to your drawings.